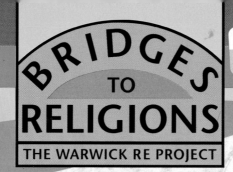

BRIDGES
TO
RELIGIONS
THE WARWICK RE PROJECT

An Egg for Babcha

Written by Margaret Barratt

Series editors: Judith Everington
and Robert Jackson

Acknowledgements

Thanks are due to Oksana's family and the Ukrainian Catholic Community in Coventry; Clive Erricker; Eleanor Nesbitt; Warwickshire Education Authority for assistance with the trialling of the materials; and The St. Gabriel's Trust for financial support in using the material on in-service courses.

Thanks are due to the following for the use of original photographs: Margaret Barratt, p.10; Noel Barratt, pp.11, 12, 19; Rosemary Jackson, p.23; Eleanor Nesbitt, pp.4, 6, 7, 9, 10, 16, 21, 22; Hilary Roberts, front and back covers, pp.8, 14, 20; Peter Roberts, pp.1, 13, 15, 18; Oxford Scientific Films, p.5.

First published 1994

98 97 96 95
10 9 8 7 6 5 4 3 2

British Cataloguing in Publication Data
A catalogue record for this book is available from the British Library

ISBN 0 435 30407 0 (One each of 5 titles)
ISBN 0 435 30403 8 (5 x An Egg for Babcha, Paperback)
ISBN 0 431 07731 2 (An Egg for Babcha, Hardback)

Heinemann Educational Publishers,
A Division of Heinemann Publishers (Oxford) Ltd,
Halley Court, Jordan Hill, Oxford OX2 8EJ

OXFORD LONDON EDINBURGH
MADRID ATHENS BOLOGNA PARIS
MELBOURNE SYDNEY AUCKLAND SINGAPORE
TOKYO IBADAN NAIROBI HARARE
GABORONE PORTSMOUTH NH (USA)

Designed and typeset by Green Door Design Ltd
Illustrated by Green Door Design Ltd
Printed in Hong Kong

Contents

Special Words

Babcha (Pronounced <u>bab</u>-cha)
'Granny' in Ukrainian

Paska (Pronounced <u>pas</u>-ka)
Sweet Easter bread

Pysanka (Pronounced pis-<u>an</u>-ka)
Special coloured egg with
patterns that give a message to
someone you love

Pysanky (Pronounced pis-<u>an</u>-kay)
More than one pysanka

What do you do at Easter?
Do you have chocolate eggs?
Do you hunt for Easter eggs in
the garden?

Easter time comes in Spring.
New leaves grow on trees and
chicks hatch from eggs.

Christians celebrate Easter in many different ways.
Louise and her friends give out flowers in church.
They decorate their Easter tree.

Douglas and his mum make an
Easter garden with a tomb.
This reminds them of Jesus in his tomb.
On Easter day they open the tomb
to show they believe Jesus is alive.

This girl is called Oksana.

She is a Christian.

Oksana's family came from
Ukraine but now they live in Britain.

This is Oksana's granny.

Oksana calls her Babcha.

Oksana loves Babcha very much.

On the Sunday before Easter, Oksana
gets pussy-willow from church.
The pussy-willow reminds her to
get ready for Easter.
She puts it behind her picture.

At Easter time Oksana's family makes special sweet bread. This special bread is called paska. They make crosses and patterns to put on the paska.

At Easter Oksana also likes to make brightly patterned eggs.
They are called pysanky.
Oksana wants to make a pysanka for Babcha to tell her she loves her.

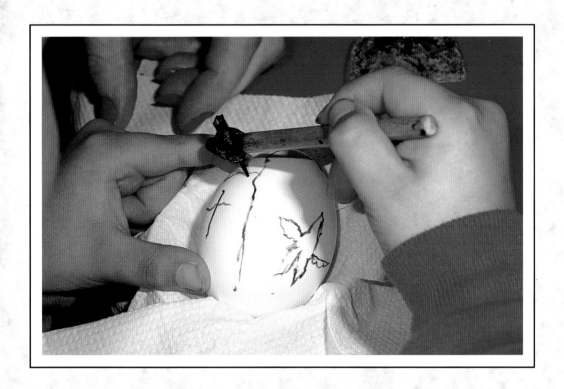

This is how Oksana and her family make pysanky.

First they take some white eggs.

Then they draw black patterns on the eggs with hot beeswax.

They put the eggs into coloured dyes.
They wait and then draw more
patterns on their eggs.
Every mark makes a good wish.

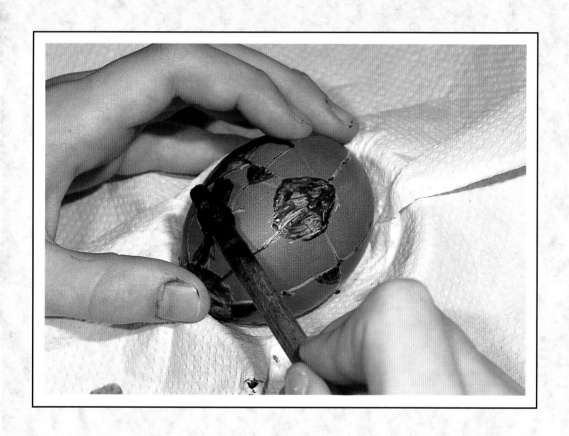

This egg looks very messy now.
Will it look beautiful when
it is finished?

Oksana carefully holds her dark
pysanka close to a candle.
The wax melts.
Little by little Oksana gently
wipes away all the wax.

Making a pysanka

1 Oksana took a special tool called a kistka.

2 The kistka filled with hot wax.

3 She drew black wax lines on her egg.

4 She put the egg into dye.

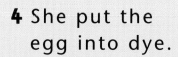

5 She did this again and again.

6 She wiped off the wax as it melted.

17

The children have all finished their beautiful pysanky.

Oksana's pysanka has a crack.

It will go bad!

Now Babcha can't have it.

Mum says, "Don't be sad.
You can give her this one.
Remember, you helped me make it."
Oksana feels much better.

Zig-zag wolves' teeth keep you safe

Pussy-willow shows Jesus went to Jerusalem

Ribbons wish you will live forever

Jesus' cross is a reminder of his love

Nets show Jesus' friends were fishermen

Spots are a reminder of Mary's tears

Isn't this pysanka lovely? All the marks on it mean something special.

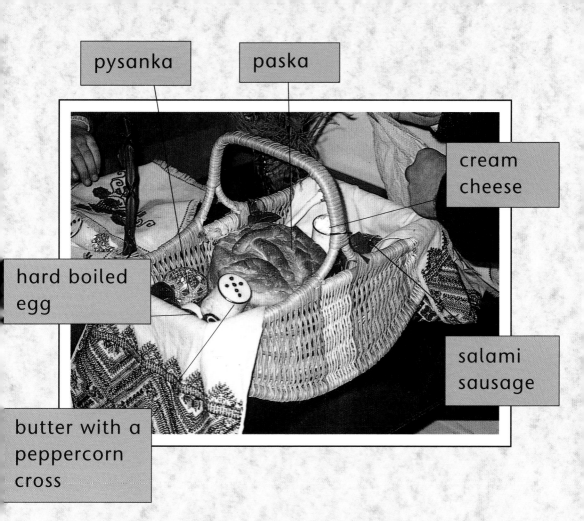

pysanka

paska

cream cheese

hard boiled egg

butter with a peppercorn cross

salami sausage

Oksana and Mum pack their Easter baskets.
The food will be blessed by the priest at church.

21

This Ukrainian writing says, "Kristos Voskres," which means "Christ is risen."

Mum gives Oksana a special Easter cover for her basket.
You can see the pictures of pysanky and willow on the cover.

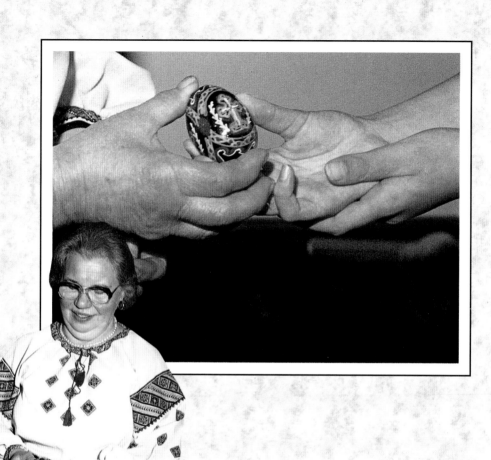

After the Easter service
Oksana gives the pysanka to Babcha.
They say "Kristos Voskres."
They will enjoy their Easter feast.

Index